Cosmological
Argument and Responses
Advanced Higher
RMPS

Laura Crichton

ISBN: 9798334471221
Imprint: Independently published, 2024

"The more that you read, the more things you will know. The more that you learn, the more places you'll go."

--Dr Seuss. A good message for Advanced Higher pupils.

CONTENTS

	Acknowledgments	i
1	Introduction	8
2	Aquinas: argument from motion, contingency, causation	Pg 12
3	Leibniz: principle of sufficient reason	Pg 23
4	Kalam argument	Pg 30
5	Philosophical responses	Pg 42
6	Scientific responses	Pg 58
7	Religious responses	Pg 68
8	Final thoughts and revision notes	Pg 72

ACKNOWLEDGMENTS

The first time I read the Cosmological Argument, I was in my first year of university in a Systematic Theology course. I remember reading it in the park on a warm, sunny day, and while that sounds idyllic, I also remember feeling like my head was going to explode. Many years later, when my then Head of Department, Gavin Park, asked/told me, "You're clever—want to teach Philosophy of Religion next year?" I accepted, firm in the knowledge I would need to start revising. I was tremendously lucky that Gavin is as geeky as I am and was happy to debate the various philosophical arguments (and many more). Through these discussions, I came to love this topic!

However, I am aware that many of my students felt the same way as I did all those years ago. I would not describe many of the textbooks 'out there' as accessible, so I set about writing my own class notes, and it's these I share with you now. I hope that you find them useful and do get in touch if you need any help.

Best wishes,

L. Crichton

1 INTRODUCTION

Let's begin by imagining a series of dominoes. If we saw them falling in sequence, we would think that something—or someone—must have knocked over the first one, starting the chain reaction. But we could also ask, who set up the dominoes in the first place? Why did they arrange them in that particular pattern? Did they stay to watch the dominoes fall, or did they run off after ruining someone else's work? The cosmological argument is concerned with questions like this (but about the universe, not dominoes) and tries to answer the question, "Why is there something rather than nothing?"

In its simplest form, the argument is often summarized like this: Everything that begins to exist has a cause, and we can trace this series of causes back through time. This series cannot go on forever because time started with the creation of the universe, and an infinite series of causes is impossible. There must have been a first cause that started everything. This cause must be outside the system of cause and effect. Traditionally, this first cause is identified as God.

However, not all cosmological arguments follow the exact same logic. Generally, cosmological arguments rely either on the principle that everything has a cause or on the idea that everything is **contingent**. In this context, contingency means that something did not have to happen and depended on something else to exist. The opposite of contingent is **necessary**. If we say that God is necessary, we mean that God must exist and cannot not exist. Other cosmological arguments say that to fully explain why everything exists, there needs to be a **sufficient reason** that explains the whole system (how and why the world came to be). Most believers accept that God created the universe out of nothing (ex nihilo), and cosmological arguments try to make sense of this belief.

Note: This is the type of language we will see in cosmological arguments, so it's important to understand what these key terms mean.

It's also useful to understand different types of arguments. The cosmological argument is *a posteriori*, which means it is based on what we can see in the world and the universe. It relies on the observation that there is a system of cause and effect, and that the universe exists. We know an *a posteriori* statement is true because we have observed it. For example, we know the sun rises every day because we have seen it happen.

The opposite is an *a priori* truth, which does not depend on experience. For example, mathematical truths like "a square has four sides" are a priori truths.

 Test your knowledge

Which of the following statements are *a posteriori* and which are *a priori*?

Tip: If you can answer the statement with "not necessarily," it's likely *a posteriori*!

1. "The sky is blue."
2. "A whole is greater than any of its parts."
3. "Water boils at 100 degrees Celsius at sea level."
4. "All bachelors are unmarried."
5. "2 + 2 = 4."
6. "Triangles have three sides."
7. "The cat is on the mat."
8. "The table is made of wood."

Checking Understanding

1. What is the cosmological argument, and what is its primary aim?

2. Define contingency and necessity within the context of the argument.

3. Explain the significance of the principle of causality in the cosmological argument.

4. Identify examples of *a posteriori* statements found within the cosmological argument. What makes them *a posteriori*?

5. Can you identify any potential strengths and weaknesses at this point? *NB – it's okay if you can't!*

2 AQUINAS

One of the most popular cosmological arguments was formulated by Saint Thomas Aquinas. We need to focus on the content of his argument, but it is interesting to also note the context. Aquinas was a Dominican friar, philosopher, theologian, and Doctor of the Church who lived in the 13th century. His observations of the world were through this particular lens—he had no awareness of scientific developments like the Big Bang—and it's wrong to think that he was trying to prove God's existence. Rather, he was attempting to find a justification for faith. Aquinas was canonized as a saint by the Catholic Church in 1323, and he is honoured as a Doctor of the Church, a title reserved for theologians whose writings have significantly contributed to Catholic doctrine and theology.

Aquinas' monumental work, the Summa Theologica, serves as a cornerstone in the history of Christian philosophy and theology. Within its pages, Aquinas meticulously constructs arguments for the existence of God, drawing upon both reason and faith. In the first three ways, collectively known as the cosmological arguments, Aquinas presents a framework grounded in observation and logic. Through these cosmological arguments, Aquinas endeavours to demonstrate the rational basis for belief in a transcendent and omnipotent Creator.

The First Way: From Motion

"It is certain, and evident to our senses, that some things are in motion. Now whatever is moved is moved by another. ...If that by which it is moved be itself moved, then this also must needs to be moved by another, and that by another again. But this cannot go on to infinity, because then there would be no first mover, and, consequently, no other movers, seeing that subsequent movers move only inasmuch as they

are moved by the first mover: as the staff moves only because it is moved by the hand. Therefore, it is necessary to arrive at a first mover, moved by no other; and this everyone understands to be God."

- Thomas Aquinas's *Summa Theologica*

Let's break this argument down a bit and think about the basis of what Aquinas was writing. Firstly, he observed 'that some things are in motion' and he acknowledged that this was 'evident to our senses.' It is therefore an a posteriori truth gained through empirical knowledge—knowledge acquired through direct observation or experience of the physical world. He further observes that there is a chain of movement that stretches through time—one thing needs to be moved by another... 'and that by another again.' However, he rejects infinity on the basis that if there were an infinite chain of movement, there would be no first mover, and therefore no subsequent movement. Given that movement does exist in the world, it would be a contradiction to say there is no first mover.

Aquinas identifies this first mover as God—but note he uses the phrase 'this everyone understands to be God.' Remember that he is writing in the 13th century where the existence of God was simply accepted. As a modern reader, if you were asked to identify an 'uncaused mover' that has a necessary existence, you may well try to identify a scientific theory that would fit. But before the advent of such discoveries, he was quite right that everyone would understand an 'unmoved mover' as God!

Notebook Task

Potentiality refers to the hidden abilities or capacities that something or someone possesses, waiting to be realized or developed. It's like the raw material or potential for change within them. Actuality, on the other hand, is the current state of existence or reality—what something or someone is actually like at this very moment. So, potentiality is what could be, while actuality is what already is.

Aquinas illustrated the concept using the analogy of fire heating wood. When fire interacts with wood, it actualizes the wood's potential to generate heat. For any transformation to occur, there must be an existing state of actuality. Without this, a thing would need to initiate its own change, necessitating simultaneous existence in both actual and potential states, which Aquinas deemed contradictory.

To put it simply, if wood could heat itself, it would already be hot. But since wood doesn't naturally have heat, it changes when fire touches it. So, the fact that wood isn't hot to start with is its current state (actuality), while its potential to get hot when fire touches it is its capability (potentiality). It cannot be in both states at once, and it cannot bring about the change by itself

For each of the following items, identify the potentiality and actuality (the first one has been done for you):

> - Ice (Potentiality: Melting into water; Actuality: Solid state of ice)
> - Seed
> - Batteries
> - Metal
> - Dough
> - Digital data
> - Students
> - Clay
> - Light bulb
> - Human body

The Second Way: From the Nature of Efficient Cause

"There is no case known (neither, indeed, is it possible) in which a thing is found to be the efficient cause of itself; for so it would be prior to itself, which would be impossible. Now in efficient causes it is not possible to go on to infinity ...Therefore it is necessary to admit a first efficient cause, to which everyone gives the name of God."

- Thomas Aquinas's *Summa Theologica*

Aquinas' second way is often grouped in with his first way as the logic may sound very familiar. In this instance, he identified a series of causes and effects in the universe. He observed that nothing can be the cause of itself, as it would have needed to exist before it existed to cause that very existence. Given that this is logically impossible, and that things do exist—he posited that

Cosmological Argument

there must be a first cause.

He again rejected the notion of infinity—so in both his first and second ways—Aquinas points to a temporal first cause; one which exists at that particular moment in time and was the initial cause of the subsequent chain. This can be referred to as an in fieri cause—for example, a spark is a 'cause *in fieri*' of a fire. However, in both of his first two ways Aquinas failed to give any reason that the cause needs to still exist—why should anyone believe that God is still around today? To truly justify faith, Aquinas needed to show that God is an *in esse* cause—one that is required for the universe's continued existence. Some people would argue that he successfully did this with his third way.

 Thinking Question

Why is it necessary for Aquinas to prove a God that is *in esse* as opposed to *in fieri*?

The Third Way: From Contingency and Necessity

"We find in nature things that are possible to be and not to be, since they are found to be generated, and to corrupt, and consequently, they are possible to be and not to be. But it is impossible for these always to exist, for that which is possible not to be at some time is not. Therefore, if everything is possible not to be, then at one time there could have been nothing in existence. Now if this were true, even now there would be nothing

in existence, because that which does not exist only begins to exist by something already existing. Therefore, if at one time nothing was in existence, it would have been impossible for anything to have begun to exist; and thus even now nothing would be in existence— which is absurd. Therefore, not all beings are merely possible, but there must exist something the existence of which is necessary. But every necessary thing either has its necessity caused by another, or not. Now it is impossible to go on to infinity in necessary things which have their necessity caused by another, as has been already proved in regard to efficient causes. Therefore we cannot but postulate the existence of some being having of itself its own necessity, and not receiving it from another, but rather causing in others their necessity. This all men speak of as God."
- Thomas Aquinas's *Summa Theologica*

This argument can also be set out as follows:

Premise (P) 1: Everything can exist or not exist; that is, everything in the natural world is contingent.

P2: If everything is contingent, then at some time there was nothing, because there must have been a time when nothing had begun to exist.

P3: If there was once nothing, then nothing could have come from nothing.

Conclusion (C) 1: Therefore, something must exist necessarily, otherwise nothing would now exist, which is absurd.

P4: Everything necessary must either have the cause of its necessity within itself or outside of itself.

P5: But the series of necessary beings cannot be infinite, or there would be no explanation of that series.

C2: Therefore, there must be some uncaused being which exists of its own necessity and sustains all other beings.

C3: And this being we all call God.

It's worthwhile revisiting what is meant by contingency and necessity at this point. As a reminder, a contingent being or event is one which is dependent on something else for its existence. Contingent events occur and then stop, and contingent objects come into being then cease to be. In a way, each of us is a contingent being because our existence only came about because of our biological parents—if prior events had been different, we may not have ever existed, and we didn't have to exist. As Parmenides wrote: "ex nihilo nihil fit," or rather, "out of nothing, nothing can come." It is not possible for us to exist without parents, just as it's not possible for something to exist out of nothingness. Of course, many accuse Aquinas of contradicting himself by saying God exists without a cause. However, this fails to understand Aquinas' third way.

Aquinas says that in order for there to be contingent events, there must be something that is—by definition—

not contingent. If everything we observe is contingent, then the explanation for the existence of the universe would seem to lie outside it. There seems to be nothing in what we observe that can explain why contingent things exist. Aquinas therefore deduces that this external reason must itself be necessary, existing outside of this system of contingency but equally being the very cause of its existence to begin with—as a sustaining cause.

By focusing on the idea of contingency, Aquinas moved away from the problems caused by time—particularly the idea that everything is simply a series of events. Imagine if time were infinite. Within infinite time, there must come a point when all contingent things cease to exist simultaneously. This concept is rooted in the notion that, with an infinite amount of time and space, every conceivable combination or eventuality would eventually manifest. Aquinas maintained that if this were the case, then a necessary being would still be required to bring everything into being, to prevent everything from ceasing to exist simultaneously, or indeed, to restart everything when that event did come about. In both finite time and infinite time, Aquinas was adamant that a necessary being was required.

Checking Understanding

1. What is the difference between an a posteriori truth and an a priori truth? Provide an example of each from the text.

2. Explain Aquinas' concept of the "first mover" in your own words. Why does he argue that an infinite regress of movers is impossible.

3. What are potentiality and actuality according to Aquinas? Provide an example not mentioned in the text to illustrate these concepts.

4. Describe the difference between an in fieri cause and an in esse cause. Why is it important for Aquinas to prove that God is an in esse cause?

5. Summarize Aquinas' third way, the argument from contingency and necessity. Why does Aquinas believe that a necessary being must exist?

Extension: Create a visual storyboard that illustrates the key points of Aquinas' three cosmological arguments.

 Past Paper Question 2019

To what extent does Aquinas offer the most convincing cosmological argument? (30)

 Past Paper Question 2021

'Aquinas' argument from motion, contingency and causation proves that God exists.' How valid is this claim? (30)

3 LEIBNIZ

IMPORTANT

There is an 'unwritten' rule, that any discussion regarding Leibniz must be accompanied by a packet of Leibniz biscuits. It is rumoured that they aid understanding – personally, I would advise the dark chocolate flavour but any are acceptable.

Leibniz was a German philosopher, mathematician, theologian, and scientist, whose achievements included the invention of calculus. Indeed, his intellect and achievements were such that they led Diderot, a later French philosopher, to remark:

"When one compares the talents one has with those of a Leibniz, one is tempted to throw away one's books and go die quietly in the dark of some forgotten corner."

Leibniz is credited with having formulated one of the most fundamental philosophical questions: 'Why is there something rather than nothing?' Although his argument is similar to Aquinas', it differs in terms of his initial observation. Instead of observing that every event has a cause, Leibniz's argument rests upon 'The Principle of Sufficient Reason'—the idea that everything has a reason why it is the way it is and why it occurred to begin with. So, if something exists or an event occurs, there must be some explanation or reason for it.

For example, if you're wondering why the sky is blue, according to this principle, there's a reason behind it. It could be because of how sunlight interacts with the

Earth's atmosphere, scattering blue light more than other colours, or it could be because you're wearing blue-tinted glasses. But the Principle of Sufficient Reason asserts that there's always a 'why' behind everything that happens or exists; there's no 'just because.' It doesn't matter what feature of the world we're talking about—if the world could have failed to be that way, then there must be some explanation of why the world is that way.

 Thinking question

Does the Principle of Sufficient Reason seem plausible to you? Can you think of any arguments against it?

Beyond the world, that is, beyond the collection of finite things, there is some One Being who rules, not only as the soul is the ruler in me, or, better, as the self is the ruler in my body, but also in a much higher sense. For the One Being who rules the universe not only rules the world but also fashions or creates it; he is above the world, and, so to speak, extramundane, and therefore he is the ultimate reason for things. For we cannot find in any of the individual things, or even in the entire collection and series of things, a sufficient reason for why they exist.

Let us suppose that a book on the elements of geometry has always existed, one copy always made from another. It is obvious that although we can explain a present copy of the book from the previous book

from which it was copied, this will never lead us to a complete explanation, no matter how many books back we go, since we can always wonder why there have always been such books, why these books were written, and why they were written the way they were. What is true of these books is also true of the different states of the world, for the state which follows is, in a sense, copied from the preceding state, though in accordance with certain laws of change. And so, however far back we might go into previous states, we will never find in those states a complete explanation for why, indeed, there is any world at all, and why it is the way it is.
  - Gottfried Wilhelm Leibniz, *Discourse on Metaphysics* or *Principles of Nature and Grace*

Leibniz's key premise seems to be that if nothing existed besides the sorts of things we find in the world, there would be no explanation of why these things exist. He uses the example of geometry books to illustrate this. Even if we can explain where each geometry book came from, we still can't explain why there are geometry books at all. And what goes for geometry books, Leibniz thinks, goes for the world as a whole. Even if we can explain how the world changes over time, we still can't explain why there is a world in the first place. Therefore, the ultimate reason why there is something rather than nothing must come from outside the world.

In the 1960s, philosophers Bertrand Russell and Frederick Copleston were involved in a famous radio debate about the existence of God and the beginning of the universe, which brought the Principle of Sufficient Reason into the spotlight. Russell argued that the universe was a 'brute fact' and that there was no need to question how the universe came into existence. He contended that while we can agree that each man has a mother, it would be illogical to say that the whole human race requires a mother—arguing that it is a different logical sphere altogether. Therefore, he found it unreasonable to demand an explanation for the existence of the entire universe.

Russell's argument challenges the Principle of Sufficient Reason by suggesting that not everything needs an explanation beyond itself. Applying this logic to Leibniz, one would argue that while Leibniz is correct in saying that each moment in time requires a cause, to assert that the whole universe must have a cause is to commit the fallacy of composition. This is akin to saying that because every brick in a building is small, the building itself must also be small.

On the other hand, Copleston defended Leibniz's Principle of Sufficient Reason by arguing that it is necessary to find an explanation for the existence of the universe. He found Russell's position frustrating, stating that 'if one refuses to even sit down at the chessboard and make a move, one cannot, of course, be check-mated.' Copleston argued that acknowledging the universe as a brute fact is an avoidance of the fundamental question: why does the universe exist?

Leibniz's Principle of Sufficient Reason thus remains a significant philosophical concept, challenging us to seek explanations for the existence of everything in the universe. The debate between Russell and Copleston illustrates the ongoing relevance and controversy surrounding this principle, and whether or not the universe requires an explanation beyond itself continues to be a central question in philosophy and theology.

 Check your understanding

1. Define the Principle of Sufficient Reason as proposed by Leibniz.
2. Explain Leibniz's analogy involving geometry books.
3. Why does Leibniz argue that the ultimate reason for the existence of the world must come from outside the world?

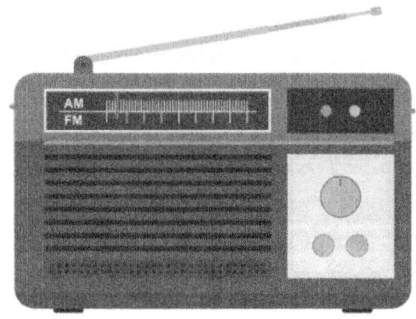

Extension: Listen to the Copleston and Russell debate (it's on youtube) and answer the following:

4. Summarize Bertrand Russell's position in his debate with Frederick Copleston regarding the explanation of the universe's existence.
5. What was Frederick Copleston's main argument in defending the Principle of Sufficient Reason during his debate with Bertrand Russell?

4 KALAM

The Kalam Cosmological Argument, arose from in the Islamic tradition from the al-Ghazali and al-Kindi scholars, but has received renewed attention from William Lane Craig in his "The Kalam Cosmological Argument (1979). In its original form, the deductive argument opens with the premise: Everything that begins to exist has a cause of its existence. The second premise follows that since the universe began to exist, it therefore, also must have had a cause[1]. From here, the Islamic scholars believed it suffice to conclude that God was the creator, and thus the explanation to our origins. However, this is an irrational jump to make, as the second premise – if accepted at all – at no point

---

[1] McGrath, A. (1999). *Science & Religion: An Introduction.* Blackwell Publishing, p.333.

implies God as the causing factor. Additionally, the possibility of an infinite universe has not yet even been ruled off the cards. Nonetheless, William Lane Craig addresses these flaws in his modified version of the argument.

In its simplest form, Craig's argument can be set forth as thus:

P1. Whatever begins to exist has a cause.

P2. The universe began to exist.

C . Therefore, the universe has a cause

This initial part of the argument hopefully feels familiar to you. We'll come to the reasons that Craig thought these premises to be *a priori* truths a little later as it's the latter part of Craig's argument which feels new: Craig argues that since the laws of nature did not exist before the universe itself, then its beginning cannot be consequence of natural laws, as there simply were none. Due to the ruling out of all-natural coincidence, the case for a personal cause is proposed. This personal cause must have openly willed to create the universe. This personal cause must have been transcendent, immanent, and omnipotent, as only a being of such stature could possibly create the universe in all its grandeur. This personal cause must have been God.[2]

> Note that the first part of the argument is **presented** as deductive – remember that this means it aims to show that the premises in the argument provide absolute support for the conclusion. The temporal argument's premises are also **presented** as *a priori* truths, meaning that they are true by definition, rather than experience. However, just because William Lane Craig presents his argument as deductive, that does not mean YOU have to accept it as such. As a deductive argument – for it to be successful, all the premises must be true and correct logic applied – so first of all, question whether he does this successfully. If you can find a premise that is *a posteriori* rather than *a priori* - you'll be some way to showing that it is inductive (and therefore could be wrong!).

Premise 1 – the causal principle

We're back to the causal principle again, which is fundamental to the majority of cosmological

---

[2] Jordan, A., Lockyer, N. and Tate, E. (2002). *Philosophy of Religion for A level*. Nelson Thornes, p.68.

arguments. As a reminder, it is the principle that asserts that every action carried out, or event that occurs, seems to be caused by a previous one - which too had a predecessor, and was part of this sequence of causation. This is relevant in relation to the universe, too, as Parmenides stated: nothing can come from nothing ("Ex nihilo, nihil fit")[3]. This chain of cause and effect has always been a constant and will continue to be so till the contingent universe is no more.

Whilst Craig is aware of the criticisms that the causal principle could be an *a posteriori* truth, Craig waves this criticism away by stating that the causal principle is "intuitively obvious" [4]. He highlights that no individual truly believes that "a horse or an Eskimo village, can just pop into being without a cause"[5].

Premise 2 – the universe began to exist

Craig aims to support the idea of a beginning by rejecting the notion of infinite universe. Again, he believes that in doing so he has provided an *a priori* truth.

---

[3] Palmer, M. (2001). *The Question of God: Introduction and sourcebook.* Routledge. P.69.
[4] Craig, W-L., Smith, Q. (1993). *Theism, Atheism, and Big Bang Cosmology.* Oxford University Press, p.147.
[5] Craig, W-L. and Sinclair, J. (2009). *The Kalam Cosmological Argument,* Blackwell Publishing, p.182.

Note that infinity can be separated into two classes: potential and actual. William Lane Craig, in his argument, encounters the latter of the two, wholly declining its possibility. An actual infinity would mean that the universe was just a beginningless sequence of events. The notion of actual infinity may seem logically possible in our minds, however, when put into practice, the concept shatters completely. Imagine it was the case that the universe was **actually** infinite. Not only would our cosmos consist of an infinite sum of objects and occurrences, but all of these would have to occur, and then cease to exist, simultaneously, as, all (limitless) possibilities would be realised instantaneously. Yet, this - in its very self - defeats the whole idea of infinity: that it is supposedly everlasting. Additionally, the idea of a universe that habitats infinite objects and events, is not of sound logic. Craig urges us to picture a fruit stall, containing an infinite supply of both apples and bananas, but also a finite collection of other, different fruits. For every apple available, there would be a banana in stock (vice-versa). Following the laws of infinity: there should be as many apples as all fruits combined; the exact amount of apples as bananas at all times (regardless of any sales made); and also an equal supply of apples and bananas together as bananas alone.[6]

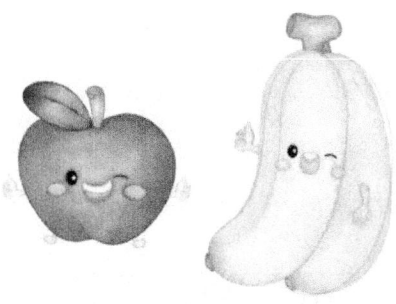

Although, it is ludicrously impossible that the total quantity of two subsets united, could equate to one, let alone the entire stock all together. Hence, actual infinity does not work when tested with reality. Furthermore, in an actual infinite universe, the fruit stall could never run out because there would always be an endless supply in existence, no matter how much was sold. Despite actual infinities maybe seeming possible in thought, they are no more than a paradox in practice.

Moreover, actual infinity cannot be reached. You cannot count to infinity: firstly, due to the absence of a starting point (zero), and secondly, since an end could

---

[6] Craig, W-L., Smith, Q. (1993). *Theism, Atheism, and Big Bang Cosmology.* Oxford University Press, p.11-16.

never be met. Although, on the other hand, Christian philosopher – Wes Morriston – questions the need to "arrive at infinity", arguing it feasible that it's just "always already there"; that we've always been (and will be) in a constant state of infinity.[7] Perhaps time is mere human invention, created to make some sense of this eternity – "from the fact that we know of no reason why something is so, it does not follow that it is impossible for it to be so".[8] Yet, just as you mathematically cannot add one to infinity, neither can successive additions be added to it, as proved earlier. An unlimited period of timeless events would remove all chronology within the universe, meaning no past, present, or future, would exist - just infinity.[9]

 Thinking question

If Craig's point is found to be valid, and that an actual infinite it impossible, then one would have to accept the conclusion that the universe began in time. But does that mean it had to have a cause? And even more so, does that cause have to be God?

---

[7] Morriston, W. (2003). *Must Metaphysical Time Have A Beginning?*. Faith and Philosophy, p.293. Available at: http://spot.colorado.edu/~morristo/metaphysical-time.pdf (accessed 10 Jan. 2018).
[8] Morriston, W. *Doubts about the Kalam Cosmological Argument.* Oxford University Press. Available at: http://spot.colorado.edu/~morristo/NewKalamCritique.pdf (accessed 10 Jan. 2018).
[9] Craig, W-L. and Sinclair, J. (2009). *The Kalam Cosmological Argument*, Blackwell Publishing, p.118.

Craig sought to answer this in the second part of his argument, Craig highlights that there are two possible reasons for why the Universes exists - a natural explanation, which means that the cause is adhering to the natural laws of nature; or a personal explanation which is due to the intentional action of a rational agent.[10] Craig makes the point that given the laws of nature came into existence at the exact same moment that the universe did, they did not exist or apply before the universe existed, hence it is reasonable to infer that it must be the result of a personal agent. The alternative is to assert that Natural Laws could preexist their own existence - which is obviously flawed logic. In Craig's mind, given the scale of the Universe, only an all-powerful being could have created it, so the personal agent pointed to by Craig could rightly be identified as God.

Further to this, given the personal agent would have to exist outside of space and time, creating the universe out of nothing, it makes sense to conclude that

---

[10] https://plato.stanford.edu/entries/cosmological-argument/#SuccAddiCannFormActuInfi 13 July 2004 : The Kalam Cosmological Argument : 6.7 - Personal Explanation : Bruce Reichenbach

something willed it to be so. The alternative is to assert that Natural Laws could pre-exist their own existence - which is obviously flawed logic.

 Thinking questions

Considering all of the arguments that Craig has put forward, which option would you support and why?

A. The universe has a beginning, but its beginning has no explanation at all.
B. The universe has a beginning, and this beginning is explained by some being outside of this finite series (i.e., God?).
C. The universe has always existed, and extends back in time infinitely, but the existence of this infinite series has no explanation at all.
D. The universe has always existed, and extends back in time infinitely, and this infinite series is explained by some being outside of the infinite series (i.e., God?).

Past Paper Question 2023: Source Question

**'Since everything that begins to exist has a cause of its existence and since the universe began to exist, we conclude that therefore the universe has a cause of its existence.'
William Lane Craig**

(a) Describe what is meant by the Kalam argument. (5)

This question isn't asking you to directly respond to the source, but it is giving you an indication of the topic. Respond to this with factual information. You should be able to do this in approximately five sentences.

(b) Analyse this source. (5)

This is asking you about the source – NOT the topic. Analysis is about thinking about the implications or potential issues that could arise. For this example, think about what you know about the Author – what potential bias could he have? What type of argumentation is being employed – does this have any potential limits? What other views might the author hold on the basis of what they have written?

(c) Evaluate this source. (5)

This question is asking you to provide a justified judgement as to whether you agree with the source. You can offer argument in both support and/or disagreement.

An answer to this question can be found on the SQA

website. The response given in the marking scheme would be given full marks.

5 PHILOSOPHICAL RESPONSES

The main philosophical criticisms come from 18th century Scottish philosopher, David Hume. In his *Dialogues Concerning Natural Religion,* he put forward a number of notable criticisms which deserved examination. To convey his arguments, Hume wrote a play in which three characters debated various arguments for the existence of God. Hume's views are thought to be represented through the character Philo - happily, for us, he raised several issues that can be applied to the versions of the cosmological argument that we have looked at.

The causal principle is suspect

The principle of sufficient reason states that nothing occurs without a sufficient reason for why it is the way it is and not otherwise i.e. everything must have a cause.

Thinking question

Is finding a sufficient reason for the existence of the universe a logical requirement? Or in other words, is it an *a priori* truth that everything must have a cause?

Option 1: The claim that everything must have a cause is true *a priori* (i.e. true by definition). Thus, denying this claim would be contradictory.

Option 2: The claim that everything must have a cause is justified *a posteriori* (i.e. it's a generalisation that fits our experiences, but which is not necessarily true). Thus, denying this claim is not in itself contradictory.

Hume opted for 'option 2' arguing that the assumption that every event must have a cause, on which the cosmological argue rests, cannot be provide. He said that this is an *a posteriori* claim: in **our experience** everything has a cause. According to Hume, there is no logical justification for saying that: 'instances of which we have had no experience, must resemble those, of which we have had experience, and the course of nature always continues the same.'

Hume asked us to imagine Adam (the first man) gazing into a pool of water and proposes that he 'could not have inferred from the fluidity and transparency of water that it would suffocate him.' His point is that you cannot look at an effect and know the true cause except through experience. One can certainly invent a cause, but this would be 'entirely arbitrary' i.e. a psychological disposition on our part. So, whilst this assumption is emotionally and intellectually reassuring but the world does not have to comply with it. Brian Magee (20th century British philosopher) picked up on this point and said that our experience simply 'forms in us the habit of expecting [a cause]' and we project this 'rule' out into the universe.

Elizabeth Anscombe, a British analytic philosopher, argued that Hume's concept of causation stems from an unreasonable sceptical view of the world. She agrees that the mind can play tricks on itself, and we may at times, misidentify a cause. But this is not to say that there isn't one. For example, imagine a magic show where the performer makes something 'disappear.' Whilst this does apparently look as if something has ceased to be – we know that in our hearts of hearts that is not the case.

It's also interesting that Hume attacked the causal principle in this way: Hume was an 'Empiricist' which means that he adopted a philosophical stance that emphasizes the role of experience and sensory perception in the acquisition of knowledge. He contended that all concepts are derived from ideas formed through sensory perception. If he said this is illogical then he would be discounting his own theories in the process. Perhaps, Hume is seeking to be deliberately obtuse through the character of Philo. But one should note that whilst the causal principle may only be an inductive generalisation, it's a strong one backed by a wealth of experience of the physical link of cause and effect. As William Lane Craig argues **"constantly verified and never falsified, the causal proposition may be taken as an empirical generalisation enjoying the strongest support experience can afford"**. Indeed, as Hume himself noted that **"I never asserted so absurd a proposition as that anything may arise without a cause"**.

The principle of sufficient reason

As we mentioned briefly before - in 1948, the BBC aired a radio debate between Frederick Copleston, a Jesuit priest and philosopher, and Bertrand Russel, a British philosopher and logician. Almost 80 years later, the debate is still referenced for its clear articulation of the arguments on both sides of the Cosmological debate and forms the basis of many of the philosophical responses explored today.

Copleston argued for the existence of God by focusing on the idea of contingency - prominent in both Aquinas' 3rd and Leibniz's versions of the Cosmological Argument – positing that everything in the world is contingent and cannot account for their own existence. Whereas Russell, argued that whilst one could not prove the non-existence of God *necessarily*, one could soundly declare that the existence of the universe is a 'brute fact' i.e., the universe is "just there, and that's all." Copleston responded scathingly by responding "If one refuses to even sit down at the chess board and make a move, one cannot, of course, be checkmated." Effectively making the point that he believed Russell was simply sticking his head in the sand and avoiding the problem of having to identify a plausible cause.

Remember that the principle of sufficient reasons states that nothing occurs with a sufficient reason for why it is and not otherwise. For example, Leibniz made the point that whilst one can create a book of geometry by copying the content from another book, that does not explain why there are geometry books to begin with. Aquinas' arguments also are dependent on this concept – questions about movement, cause and existence presuppose not only that there must be an explanation for the individual features but an explanation of why these things exist at all. Both Leibniz and Aquinas have then gone beyond the world of contingent things to find an a 'complete' answer for this. As Copleston phrased it 'an adequate explanation must ultimately be a total explanation, to which nothing further can be added.'

Russell responded to Copleston by saying 'then I can only say that you're looking for something which can't be got, and which one ought not to expect.' However, Russell's point isn't simply that it is practically impossible to find an answer, but also that by following a chain back through time, you are only ever going to end up with a nonsensical solution. For example, I could ask why you chose to study this particular topic at school.

You might respond by outlining your personal motivations and the subject's relevance in the wider world, or you could point to the requirements of the national exam board. But if I kept asking 'why why why' pulling you all the way back through history, we wouldn't actually find an answer to you choosing the study the cosmological argument. The answer to my question would be unsatisfactory because your response would be so obscure.

Logicians – such as Russell – call this weakness the **'fallacy of composition'**. This fallacy consists in claiming that, since every member of the class has a certain property, the class has a whole has the same property. As Russell proposed to Copleston:

'I can illustrate what seems to me your fallacy. Every man who exists has a mother and it seems to be your argument is that therefore the human race must have a mother, but obviously the human race hasn't a mother – that's a different logical sphere.'

Essentially Russell contended that as the universe is simply a name given to a collection of parts, if we have explained each and every part, then it is not necessary to the explain the whole. David Hume too, picked up on this criticism arguing 'Did I show you the particular causes of each individual in a collection of twenty particles ot matter, I should think it very unreasonable, should you afterwards ask me, what was the cause of the whole twenty.'

Thinking questions – who has the strongest argument?

Do proponents of the cosmological argument really commit the fallacy of composition?

- Imagine a simple red brick wall. Each brick in the wall is small. If we apply the same logic as Aquinas in relation to contingency, we must conclude that the wall is also small. After all, the wall is simply a name given to a collection of bricks stacked in a particular way!
- But is a wall simply a collection of bricks? Not necessarily – walls can also contain cement and other decorative features. Even if we were to apply the characteristics of the component parts to the whole, is this always wrong? Going back to the wall analogy, imagine if every brick were destroyed – it would be reasonable to say that the wall has also been destroyed. Surely the same could be said for the universe - if every contingent being in the universe ceased to exist, would the universe still exist?
- Can argue that the 'universe' is more than a collection of contingent events? The universe is not merely a conglomeration of physical bodies but also the space and time in which they exist and the laws according to which they operate, the universe is in fact one of those bodies whose existence as a whole is distinct from the existence of its parts. Consequently, is it not entirely coherent to assert that the whole of the universe

remains unexplained, even where every one of its constituent physical parts is accounted for?
- One could also ask whether Russell and Copleston are asking the same kind of question. There is a difference between asking how something works and asking why it works that way. For example, I could ask why Freddie has forgotten his homework. One could look for a concrete reason – he left it on the dining table, but one could also look for a purposeful reason – he was up late watching endless Tiktok videos and was too tired to remember everything. Both answers are legitimate responses to the question – are they equally valid?

An infinite regress is perfectly possible

One of the key ideas behind cosmological arguments is that there can't be an endless series of events stretching back into the past – or rather, that an infinite series of events is impossible.

However, not all philosophers agree with this conclusion.

Hume argued that proponents (such as Aquinas) wrongly assume a *simultaneous* ceasing of all contingent things. He argued that the overlapping existence of contingent beings means that it is not necessary for all things to have ceased to exist at any given moment. He suggested that if time were infinite, then every event, including the existence of contingent beings, could have occurred at various points along that infinite timeline, without necessitating a first cause.

To explain this further, we can create our own analogy. Imagine we flip a coin – heads means existence and tails means non-existence. There's 50/50 chance between the two options. But if we were to ask the entire class to flip coins, then the odds that all the coins would land on heads becomes more interesting. Now imagine the whole school are flipping coins. Then the whole of Edinburgh. Then Scotland. Then the UK. Then the world. The chances of *all* coins landing on heads greatly diminishes. Aquinas would argue that this changes within an *actual infinite:* no matter how many coins there are, within infinite time, with an infinite number of simultaneous coin flips, all coins will land on tails at the same time. So again, either time is not infinite or there is a necessary being stopping this from occurring. However, with infinite coin flips, you will almost surely see at least one result of heads, that is, the probability that you get at least one heads is 1. There is, however, the possible situation where you get an infinite sequence of tails - it's not explicitly impossible for this to happen. But, since there are an infinite number of sequences that have at least one head, and only one sequence with no heads, the probability of getting that infinite sequence of tails is $1/X$ in the limit of X going to infinity, which is 0.

Equally, we could go with Hume and say that Aquinas has misrepresented events – we can accept that contingent things begin and end – but it wrong to believe they do so simultaneously. We can accept logically the universe (as a collective noun for all contingent things) is also contingent. But we must also consider how those within the collection function. Contingent events overlap, so there is nothing to say that these could not simply go on overlapping for infinite time. Hume would argue that we do not need a beginning, or an explanation, if events have simply occurred in this overlapping fashion – for an infinite existence.

It occurs to me, that whilst we often let Aquinas 'off the hook' for not considering modern scientific discovery, we rarely extend that same courtesy to Hume. All of our current scientific theory supports the idea that time did 'begin' at the moment of the Big Bang – in that it is a separate dimension that came into being at that moment. Which would support Aquinas' proposition – but on a point of philosophy? Who wins?

William Lane Craig – as a 21st century philosopher – has the advantage of being aware of science, but still sought to reject infinite on a philosophical basis (to be fair he is a theologian not a scientist!) He also used an analogy: he asks us to imagine a library with an infinite number of books, half of which are red. According to

Craig, halving infinity doesn't make it smaller; it's still infinity. This might seem logical in theory, but Craig argues it creates problems when applied to reality. In this scenario, the set of red books would seem smaller than the set of all books. Yet paradoxically, both sets are considered infinite. Craig concludes that if infinities could be both smaller than and the same size as other infinities, then they cannot **actually** exist.

Mathematician David Hilbert devised a thought experiment to illustrate the problem with 'actual infinites' – this is often referred to simply as 'Hilbert's hotel.' He asked us to imagine a hotel with an infinite number of rooms, each room numbered with positive integers (1, 2, 3, and so on). Despite having infinitely many rooms, the hotel is fully occupied; every room has a guest.

Now, suppose a new guest arrives and wants a room. Since there are infinitely many rooms, the hotel manager can easily accommodate this new guest by shifting every current guest to the room with the number one higher than their current room. In other words, the guest in room 1 moves to room 2, the guest in room 2 moves to room 3, and so on. This shift creates a vacancy in room 1 for the new guest.

But what if an infinite busload of new guests arrives? The hotel manager can still accommodate them all. He simply asks each current guest to move to the room whose number is double their current room number. For example, the guest in room 1 moves to room 2, the guest in room 2 moves to room 4, the guest in room 3 moves to room 6, and so on. This doubling ensures that an infinite number of rooms become vacant, allowing the new guests to be accommodated.

The paradoxical aspect of Hilbert's Hotel is that even though it's already full, it can always make room for more guests. This demonstrates the counterintuitive nature of infinite sets, where operations such as addition and multiplication behave differently than they do with finite sets. However, this seeming absurdity arises primarily from applying finite set intuitions to infinite sets. Mathematician Georg Cantor argued that infinite sets possess distinct properties, including the possibility of one-to-one relations with their subsets, challenging traditional notions of size and comparison. Craig takes it to be obviously absurd for a subset (red books) to be both smaller than and equal to its set (all the books). However, it's only absurd for finite sets. For infinite sets it's not absurd, it's actually their defining characteristic. When we think of libraries or hotels, we have in mind our ideas about finite sets of things, but

Cantor argued such intuitions are not applicable to infinite sets. Infinite sets simply have different mathematical properties, one of which is the possibility of a one-to-one relation between the number of members of infinite sets and those of their subsets.

Why must the necessary being be God?

You'll recall that William Lane Craig tried to prove that the universe's "first cause" must be a personal creator, like God. He argued that because the laws of nature didn't exist before the universe began, the universe couldn't have come from natural causes. In other words, before the universe started, there were no physical laws or processes that could have caused it. Craig said, *"if the universe began to exist, and if the universe is caused, then the cause of the universe must be a personal being who freely chooses to create the world."* This means he believes a personal being, like God, made a conscious decision to create the universe.

Hume challenged Craig's idea. He suggested that if we can accept that some things (like God) exist without needing an explanation, then why can't the universe itself be one of those things? Hume asked, "Why may not the material universe be the necessarily existent Being, according to this pretended explication of necessity?" This means he was questioning why the universe itself couldn't just exist without needing a cause.

Hume also made another point: trying to find answers outside the universe only leads to more questions we can't answer. He said, "When you go one step beyond the mundane system, you only excite an inquisitive humour, which it is impossible ever to satisfy." In simpler terms, he meant that looking beyond the universe for answers doesn't help because we can't observe or understand anything outside the universe. We'll just end up with more questions and no real answers.

Immanuel Kant (German philosopher) also made this point – he raised the point that any *a posteriori* argument is limited by our experiences within the world that we can observe i.e. what we sense and observe. Kant asserted that we cannot use what we see in the natural world, to then make claims about the supernatural world. As the causal principle operates *in* the universe, it cannot advance us beyond it and therefore is not useful when trying to prove a supernatural God.

Activity idea

At this point in the course, I usually hold a 'philosopher's tea party.' Each student is assigned a role in advance e.g. Hume, Copleston, Russell, Craig, Aquinas, Leibniz, Anscombe etc. They then spend time researching and revising their assigned philosophers' arguments, key points, and historical context. The following lesson we then set about and have a debate over cups of tea.

One year, everyone also brought food items relating to their characters e.g. Italian Biscotti for Aquinas, Battenberg cake (it reminded them of a chess board from Copleston, stale bread for Hume (he is quite miserable). Another year, people went a little overboard on props – there were some fantastic hats! My absolute favourite was the pupil who came as Bertrand Russel with a Bubble Pipe (google his picture if this doesn't make sense). The aim is to make it memorable, but you do need to come prepared!!

However, I'm aware some of you will be learning this alone, therefore you might wish you write your own play (inspired by Hume) and this could be set wherever you want. Whatever the location, I would still advise snacks.

 Past Paper Question 2022

To what extent is Leibniz's argument from the principle of sufficient reason successful?

6 SCIENTIFIC RESPONSES

Quantum Theory

As William Lane Craig asserted the Causal Principle is considered 'intuitively obvious', as it's based on our everyday experiences and scientific observations that suggest things don't just pop into existence without a cause. The idea is that something cannot come from nothing.

However, the Causal Principle has faced significant criticism, especially from the perspective of quantum physics. On the quantum level, the connection between cause and effect, if not entirely broken, is to some extent loosened. For example, it appears that electrons can pass out of existence at one point and come back into existence elsewhere. One can neither trace their intermediate existence nor determine what causes them to come into existence at one point rather than another. Neither can one precisely determine or predict where they will reappear; their subsequent location is only statistically probable given what we know about their antecedent states. In other words, **Quantum Physics** suggests that something <u>can</u> come out of nothing.

William Lane Craig responds that appeals to quantum phenomena do not affect the *kalam* argument (although this has already been found lacking). He argues that **"quantum events are not completely devoid of causal conditions"**. Just because quantum events <u>look</u> uncaused doesn't mean that they are. Furthermore, quantum events are only known to occur in the contingent universe, which is ruled by causal conditions, meaning even the most spontaneous events - such as these - are still governed by the causal principle. There is also a substantial difference between electrons passing out of existence, and the entirety of the universe coming into being.

However, Stephen Hawking disagreed with this assessment explaining in his posthumous book, "Since we know the universe itself was once very small- perhaps smaller than a proton- this means something quite remarkable. It means the universe itself in all it's mind-boggling vastness and complexity, could simply have popped into existence without violating the known laws of nature."[11]

---

[11] Stephen Hawking. Brief Answers to the Big Questions. (London: John Murray, 2018). 34

Thinking question

How might Aquinas respond to this theory?

The Big Bang

Whilst people may think of science and religion in opposition to each other, that is not always the case. Arguably, the Big Bang theory can support cosmological arguments by marking the universe's beginning.

The Big Bang Theory maintains that the universe began around 13-14 billion years ago in a unique, non-temporal event. Something, maybe a quantum vacuum, appeared and rapidly expanded, creating the universe we experience today. This process happened in the first tiny fraction of a second, and although it's still debated how exactly it occurred, the key idea is that the universe had a beginning. Even today, the universe is expanding, with galaxies moving away from each other. If we look back in time, the universe gets smaller and eventually reaches a point of infinite density and gravitational force. This point is called a singularity and represents the beginning of everything: matter, energy, space, time, and physical laws. The research of 'dark energy' have further supported this. Dark energy makes up approximately 68% of the universe[12] and is responsible for the repulsive force that has led to the expansion of the universe. It is, therefore, reasonable to infer that if the distance between galaxies is increasing, they must have been closer together further back in time, which supports the idea of a space-time singularity and hence the Big Bang Theory.

There was no "before" this point because time itself started with the Big Bang.

 Thinking question

If all laws began at the moment of the Big Bang – is there any logic in asking what caused it to happen?

Some scientists argue that the Big Bang isn't an "event" in the usual sense. As Hawking notes, **"the finite universe has no space-time boundaries and hence lacks singularity and a beginning. And without a beginning the universe requires no cause."** The best one can say is that the universe is finite with respect to the past, not that it was an event with a beginning." In other words, events happen within space and time, but the Big Bang didn't have a space-time context. There was no time before the Big Bang and no space in which it occurred. Therefore, it can't be considered a physical event that happened at a specific time – and

---

[12] 'Dark Matter' <https://home.cern/science/physics/dark-matter> [Accessed 1 December 2018]

therefore does not require a cause.

In response, one could therefore reformulate the Cosmological argument as follows:

P1. If something has a finite past, it must have a cause.

P2. The universe has a finite past.

C1. Therefore, the universe must have a cause.

P4. Since space-time started with the universe and has a finite past, the cause must exist outside space and time.

P6. If the cause exists outside space-time, scientific explanations (based on physical laws) can't explain the universe's origin.

C2. If no scientific explanation can explain the universe's origin, the cause must be a personal agent (like God).

However, critics say that just because something is finite doesn't mean it needs a cause. Adolf Grünbaum - who was particularly well-known for his work on the philosophy of space and time – argued that events only result from other events. Since the Big Bang singularity isn't a real event and the starting point (t=0) isn't a genuine moment in time, the singularity can't have a cause. Therefore, the singularity t=0 cannot be the effect of any cause, whether it's an event-cause or an agent-cause.

Modern physics tells us that time isn't something the

universe sits in but a part of the universe itself, linked with space and matter through relativity. So, outside the universe, there's no time. If we could view the universe from outside, time would just be one of its internal features, not something that applies externally. This means saying the universe "began to exist" like a physical object doesn't make sense. There could be a first moment of time, but this isn't a true "beginning" like we think of objects starting or stopping within time.

So, the idea that "everything which begins to exist has a cause" doesn't work here because the universe didn't begin in that way. The universe's "age" is about its internal timeline, not its existence in extemporal existence. This idea is compatible with the universe having a finite internal time.

 Thinking Question

If we understand time as an internal feature of the universe – what impact does this have on **temporal** Cosmological arguments?

The Conservation of Mass-Energy

Even if we were to accept that the Big Bang requires a cause we are still left with the need to make an abductive judgement as to which is more likely - did God cause the Big Bang or was it a much simpler Non-event?

However, the Principle of Conservation of Mass-Energy arguably can provide an answer to this question. This principle dictates that mass and energy can never be created or destroyed rather they simply transmute into one another.

I like to think about this in relation to the circle of life – when we die whilst our form may change, we might be buried and decay – but this is simply the point our energy is transferred (or transmuted) into another form. For example, we then see that plants use this energy to grow within graveyards. Those then put oxygen into the air allowing the continued survival of other forms etc. etc. So, our forms maybe contingent, but our continued existence is necessary.

Mass and energy are not contingent on anything - they remain as a constant - and as a result, it means they require no cause and thus it is likely that they have always existed as they cannot be created. Mass and energy can exist outwith time as their existence is not contingent upon it. Therefore, the existence of the material universe can be ascribed to the transmutations of energy into matter. The implication of this is that mass-energy effectively becomes the necessary being of all material aspects of the universe, which theists originally proclaimed was God. In effect, we are all necessary beings.

 Thinking question

Which part of the Cosmological Argument is most damaged by this theory? Is there any defence against it?

Oscillating Universe Theory

I'm loathed to include this 'theory' in a chapter on science, but pupils seem to like it and it does appear in a lot of essays.

The theory was first suggested by Russian scientist Alexander Friedmann between 1922 and 1924. Three years later, it did received some support from Hungarian scientist Cornelius Lanczos who also published a paper on the idea. However, by 1934, American physicist Richard Tolman showed through his work that the oscillating model had significant issues and it hasn't seen any significant revival since.

Essentially the theory proposed the universe be in an infinite loop, expanding and contracting repeatedly. This means there might have been multiple Big Bangs in the past and could be more in the future. The current universe could be a "reboot" of earlier ones that expanded and then contracted. This is sometimes referred to as a "big crunch."

We don't have any physical laws that explain how the universe could go through endless cycles of collapsing and exploding again. Just because the universe expanded once doesn't mean it can keep doing so. Even if it did, the cycles wouldn't be regular. With each cycle, entropy (disorder) would increase, making each new cycle longer than the last. If the universe had no beginning and has been cycling forever, the current cycle would be infinitely long, which isn't the case.

Additionally, if the universe were to be in an infinite cycle of 'crunch' and 'bang' again, the radiation would keep adding up. Because we measure a specific amount of cosmic background radiation, we can infer that the universe could only have gone through a finite number of cycles—no more than 100. This means the universe can't be cyclical infinitely.

Recent discoveries also challenge the idea of an oscillating universe. Observations of distant supernovae show that the universe's expansion is speeding up. These supernovae are dimmer than expected, suggesting they are farther away, which means the expansion has accelerated over billions of years. This acceleration makes it unlikely that the universe will ever collapse and cycle again.

 Thinking question

If found to be true, what impact would this theory have on the cosmological argument?

 Past Paper Question 2021

'Scientific responses to the cosmological argument show that it is unsuccessful.' How valid is this claim?

 Past Paper Question 2023

'The best one can say is that the universe is finite with respect to the past, not that it was an event with a beginning.'

To what extent do you agree with scientific responses to the cosmological argument? (30)

Cosmological Argument

7 RELIGIOUS RESPONSES

Given that cosmological arguments tend to come from 'religious' people, it's hard to imagine a 'religious response' that is anything but applause and agreement. God in the Christian Bible is depicted in many ways, showing different aspects of His character and nature and these align with the Cosmological argument neatly:

Creator: The Cosmological Argument posits that the universe had a beginning and therefore must have a cause. This aligns with the depiction of God as the Creator in the Bible, who brought everything into existence from nothing (Genesis 1:1).

All-Powerful (Omnipotent): To cause the universe, this being must have immense power. The sheer scale and complexity of the universe imply that its cause must be all-powerful, reinforcing the biblical attribute of God's omnipotence (Jeremiah 32:17).

All-Knowing (Omniscient): Creating a universe with intricate laws of nature, precise conditions for life, and immense complexity suggests that the cause has incredible knowledge. This supports the idea of God being all-knowing, as depicted in the Bible (Psalm 147:5).

All-Present (Omnipresent): The argument suggests that the first cause exists outside of time and space, indicating that this being is not confined by the physical universe. This supports the idea of God being omnipresent, as He is not limited by physical dimensions (Jeremiah 23:24).

Loving: While the Cosmological Argument itself doesn't directly argue for God's love, the idea that God created the universe with conditions suitable for life and human existence can be seen as an act of love and care, which aligns with biblical teachings (John 3:16).

Just: The idea of a rational and purposeful creator supports the concept of a moral order in the universe, which is foundational for justice. This correlates with the biblical view of God as just and righteous (Psalm 11:7).

Merciful: The argument doesn't directly address mercy, but if the creator is a personal being who desires a relationship with creation, it aligns with the biblical depiction of God's mercy and willingness to forgive (Ephesians 2:4-5).

Holy: The first cause being outside of the physical universe suggests purity and separateness from the material world, which supports the idea of God's holiness (Isaiah 6:3).

Personal: The Cosmological Argument, especially in Craig's version, posits that the cause of the universe is a personal agent with the intention to create. This supports the biblical depiction of God as personal and relational, desiring a relationship with humans (Matthew 6:9).

However, you should remember that St. Thomas Aquinas wasn't attempting to prove the existence of God but rather to justify his faith. It should come as no surprise, therefore, that if found successful, the Cosmological Argument aligns rather neatly with the Christian understanding of God. If you are asked to write an essay that specifically focuses on 'religious responses' to the Cosmological Argument, then I would suggest that you acknowledge Aquinas' faith and explore ways that his arguments can be defended in the face of other criticisms. For example, the Big Bang Theory seems to provide a cause, but Aquinas could argue that this is God because the Bible teaches that He is the beginning. While the Conservation of Mass-Energy may provide a plausible alternative to God as a necessary being, this also fits with the Christian idea that we are all one with God through baptism, and our being linked in this way supports that ideal. I know that this is dependent on having a good knowledge of Christianity, but as many of you will have studied this topic at Higher, you may well have the knowledge already.

8 FINAL THOUGHTS AND REVISION NOTES

My final thoughts on this topic, actually come from one of my former pupils – Lesley-Ann Armitage:

Perhaps the answer to any of these questions will never truly be attained and therefore all justifications are mere speculation. When being inquisitive about the origins of our universe or purpose of humankind, the discovery or self-realisation of one's surroundings can ground us into our state of humanity. Comparatively, we are insignificant creatures, who if our history and evolution had been altered even in the slightest would have not evolved in such a way that we are the top of the natural hierarchy.

I rather liked her acknowledgment that even if we can never discover the truth to these philosophical questions – we can still see the value in pursuing answers and that there can be benefits to doing so that are entirely separate to the answers we seek.

 Source Questions

The following sources were provided by the SQA to help pupils to practice.

"If at one time nothing was in existence, it would have been impossible for anything to have begun to exist; and even now nothing would be in existence." *Thomas Aquinas*

- a) Describe Aquinas' argument from motion, contingency, causation. (5)
- b) Analyse this source. (5)
- c) Evaluate this source. (5)

"Every being which begins has a cause for its beginning; now the world is a being which begins; therefore, it possesses a cause for its beginning." *Al-Kindi*

- a) Describe the Kalam argument. (5)
- b) Analyse this source. (5)
- c) Evaluate this source. (5)

"Something exists rather than nothing because a necessary being exists which carries within itself the reason for existence and is the sufficient reason for the existence of all contingent being." *Gottfried Leibniz*

- a) Describe Leibniz's argument for sufficient reason. (5)
- b) Analyse this source. (5)
- c) Evaluate this source. (5)

"The universe is just there, and that's all" *Bertrand Russell*

a) Describe the Cosmological Argument. (5)
b) Analyse this source. (5)
c) Evaluate this source. (5)

"Such a cause must be beginningless and uncaused... Ockham's Razor will shave away further causes, since we should not multiply causes beyond necessity. This entity must be unimaginably powerful, since it created the universe out of nothing." *William Lane Craig*

a) Describe the Kalam Argument. (5)
b) Analyse this source. (5)
c) Evaluate this source. (5)

Revision notes

Some of the points below summarise the notes from this book, whereas others indicate thinkers/ideas that you may want to look at in class or as part of your own study. Remember, at Advanced Higher level, although there are mandatory bullet points there is a lot of freedom within those to examine any number of thinkers.

About the argument
- The argument states that the universe requires a cause and an explanation: God.
- **'Cosmological'** comes from cosmos (Greek for world); it is concerned with the cause of the world.

- The argument is **a posteriori** (based on experience), **inductive** (probabilistic) and **synthetic** (requiring evidence, not purely logical).
- Perhaps the first cosmological argument was that of the ancient Greek philosopher **Aristotle,** who claimed that there must be a 'Prime Mover' – the original source of motion in our world.

Thomas Aquinas
- **13th century** theologian from Italy.
- Aquinas looks back to Aristotle.
- He gives three cosmological arguments.
- These form the first three of his famous Five Ways – five proofs for God.

First Way
Change (Motion)

P1) Potentially, anything could exist.
P2) Some things actually exist.
P3) If P. changes* to A. then outside force was applied to P.
P4) The universe (Pu) actually exists (A).

---

c) An outside force was applied (God)

Second Way
Causality
P1) If a thing exists in the universe, it must have a prior cause.
However,

Pa) If C&E went back endlessly, universe would never have started
Pb) The universe did start
___

c) C&E chain did not go back endlessly
P2) The universe exists
___

Third Way
Contingency
P1) If something exists "contingently" (i.e. it may just as easily not exist), it needs a non-contingent cause to start it off.
P2) The universe exists contingently
P3) "God" has "necessary existence".
___

c) God must have been the necessary cause of our contingent universe.
C+) Therefore God must exist.

Leibniz - Principle of Sufficient Reason
P: For everything that exists there must be a sufficient reason to account for its existence
P: The world exists, but contains no sufficient explanation within it for this existence
P: The explanation for the world must lie outside of it
C: The sufficient explanation must be God

Frederick Copleston
Copleston borrows from both Aquinas' 3rd way and Leibniz
P: Everything in the universe is contingent

P: Contingent things do not act as a sufficient explanation for their own existence
P: The universe, because it is contingent, cannot contain anything that explains its own existence
P: There must be a necessary being outside the universe that constitutes a sufficient reason for the universe's existence
C: This necessary being is God

Kalam Argument
Al Ghazali & Al Kindi (801-873AD)
- Argued that **actual infinities** are **impossible**
- P: Nothing that exists can cause itself
- P: The world exists
- P: The world must have been caused
- C: This cause was God

William Lane Craig (current)
- The universe had a beginning.
- That beginning was caused.
- **That cause was probably personal** (making the choice to create).
- Therefore God exists.

Hume's Criticisms
- We can make assumptions about cause and effect that might be wrong
- We have developed habits of seeing causes and effects that are not necessarily logical

- Is it not necessary for the whole universe to have a cause, just because everything within it can be explained with reference to a preceding cause
- "Just because every human has a mother, does not mean the entire human race has a mother." Bertrand Russell

Criticisms of Aquinas 1st & 2nd Ways
- **The possibility of infinite regress** (Aquinas rejects with little justification
- **Bertrand Russell** - the earth is a 'brute fact' with no need for explanation, to attempt to explain
- it is to give unnecessary meaning to the world.
- **The inductive leap** - Aquinas jumps from inferring that there must be a first cause to the idea that this is the God of Classical Theism.
- **Contradiction** - Aquinas argues that everything needs a prior cause, and then contradicts this by arguing for the uniqueness of God
- **Plurality of Causes** - perhaps there are many causes of the world, or an imperfect cause (**Hume**)
- **Kant** - Causality may simply be something imposed on experiences by the mind, it is not real.

Criticisms of Aquinas' 3rd Way
- The notion of a necessary being is a logical impossibility, from our experience
- If we assign 'necessity' as a characteristic to God, we are no longer presenting an a posteriori argument

- The idea of an *a priori* being is unverifiable and beyond what we know
- Aquinas' argument relies on the belief rather than demonstration that infinite regress is impossible

Criticism of the Kalam
- The challenge of **quantum physics** – according to quantum physicists, something can come from nothing (electrons passing in and out of existence without any prior cause). This contradicts the first premise of the argument ("nothing comes from nothing").
- The **oscillating universe** theory – some physicists maintain that the world never "began" as such – the universe is part of an infinite process of expansion and collapse.
- The **Big Bang** as an alternative explanation – did the universe come about as a result of the clashing of sub-atomic matter? If so the idea of a creator God becomes less relevant!
- The Universe might not have involved a deliberate choice - it may have been **entirely impersonal.**

Useful Quotes

Bertrand Russell "Just because every human has a mother, does not mean the entire human race has a mother"

Bertrand Russell "The universe is just there, and that's all there is to say."

Frederick Coppleston "There needs to be a necessary being to explain why everything else exists. Contingent beings (like everything we know in the universe) lack the 'sufficient reason' to explain why they exist"

Gottfried Leibniz "If you suppose the world eternal, you will suppose nothing but a succession of states, and will not find in any a sufficient reason to account for it's existence"

Swinburne "There could be no simpler explanation than one which postulates only one cause. Theism is simpler than polytheism."

Other reading

Particularly if you have chosen to study the cosmological argument for your dissertation, the following sources may be of use.

William Lane Craig and Quentin Smith. *Theism, Atheism and Big Bang Cosmology.* (New York: Oxford University Press, 1993)

William Lane Craig. *The Kalam Cosmological Argument.* (Eugene: Wipf and Stock, 2000)

Michael Palmer. *The Question of God.* (Abingdon, Routledge, 2001)

Hans Reichenbach. *The Rise of Scientific Philosophy.* (California, University of California Press, 1961) p208

Richard Swinburne. *The Existence of God.* (Oxford, Oxford University Press, 2004 2nd Edition)

Mel Thompson. *Philosophy of Religion.* (London: Teach Yourself, 2010)

Peter Vardy. *The Puzzle of God.* (London, Fount Paperbacks, 1999 Revised Edition)

Stanford Encyclopaedia of Philosophy; 'Cosmological Argument'
<http://plato.stanford.edu/entries/cosmological-argument/>

OTHER BOOKS IN THE ENLIGHTENED RMPS COLLECTION

National 5: Judaism

National 5: Existence of God

Higher: Islam

Advanced Higher: Teleological Argument

Advanced Higher: Atheism

Advanced Higher: Medical Ethics

All available on Amazon.

You can also find us on Instagram (@enlightenedrmps)

ABOUT THE AUTHOR

Laura Crichton is a teacher of Religious, Moral, and Philosophical Studies in Edinburgh. She gained her MA in Divinity at the University of Aberdeen, before completing her PGDE at the University of Edinburgh. She has taught Advanced Higher RMPS since 2009 and works for the Scottish Qualifications Authority - at both Higher and Advanced Higher. Before teaching, she served in the Royal Signals Corps and now is a CCF Army Officer. She enjoys teaching immensely - provided she has a cup of coffee in hand.

Printed in Great Britain
by Amazon